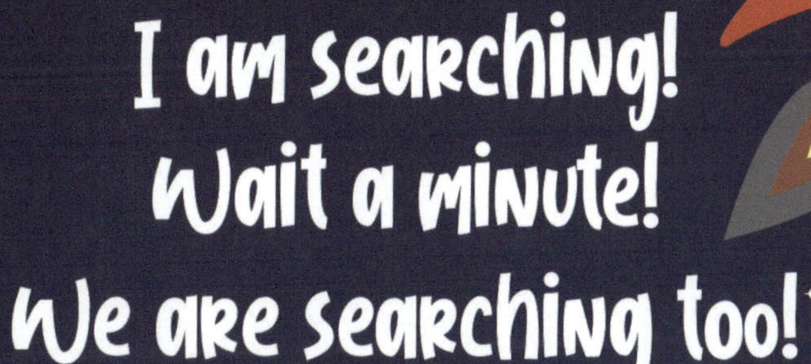

Zabed Mohammad, PhD.
Educator & Researcher
Canada

Edited by
Robert Hart

Editorial Assistants
Zarir Shiddike

Kids Edu Care

Library of Congress Cataloging-in-publication Data
ISBN: 978-1-7388326-5-1

Publisher: Kids Edu Care Inc.
Children's Dedicated Learning Series
Website: www.kidseducare.ca
Illustration Copyright © 2022 by
Kids Edu Care Inc.

Illustration & Design
Bee Digital

This book belongs to

....

....

Kids Edu Care

I can search for God's existence.
Because...I live in the 21st Century!

Can we try to search...
To find God/Allah?
Is there anyone
who has tried
before?

That's a good question!
Do you know...
The Prophet and Messenger
Ibrahim (AS)?

Prophet Ibrahim's father's name was Azar.
He was born in what is now IRAQ!
Tehr
Hamadan
Kermanshah
Tigris
o r o t a
m i a
SYRIA
Euphrates
IRAQ
Baghdad
Damascus
Syrian
Desert

Since childhood
He was so curious.
Like you and all other
curious children!

One day,
at a very young age,
He started to search for
God/Allah!

One night
He saw a shining STAR!
It was the biggest and
brightest in the sky.
He thought, Wow!

The star has light and it removes
the darkness of night.
He said, "This must be God/Allah!"

After some time
The star went away!
He could no longer find
the star in the sky.
He was stuck!!

Ibrahim (AS) started to think.
He knew that God would
never go away, so...
He came to a decision
and said..."No, No, No!
The star is not God/Allah!"

Ibrahim (AS) then saw the MOON.
It was now brightest and removed
the darkness at night.
Ibrahim (AS) said,
"This is my God/Allah!"

Then the MOON disappeared!
Ibrahim (AS) again thought
as the moon went away,
"This cannot be God/Allah.
Because...
God would never go away!"

Ibrahim (AS) continued
searching for God/Allah.
He saw the SUN in the sky...
The sun filled the sky with
its bright glow.
Ibrahim (AS) was
extremely happy.

Ibrahim (AS) felt so happy
Because...
He again thought
he had found God.
In the SUN,
the greatest star of all!

As time passed, the day came to an end.
The sun began to set in the west.
When the sun disappeared from the sky...
The world sank into deep darkness.

Ibrahim (AS) again thought,
Something came, "but went away again!
It appeared and disappeared!
It cannot be God/Allah!"

Then, he thought,
Who controls them?
How do they appear?
Why do they disappear?
Who created them?

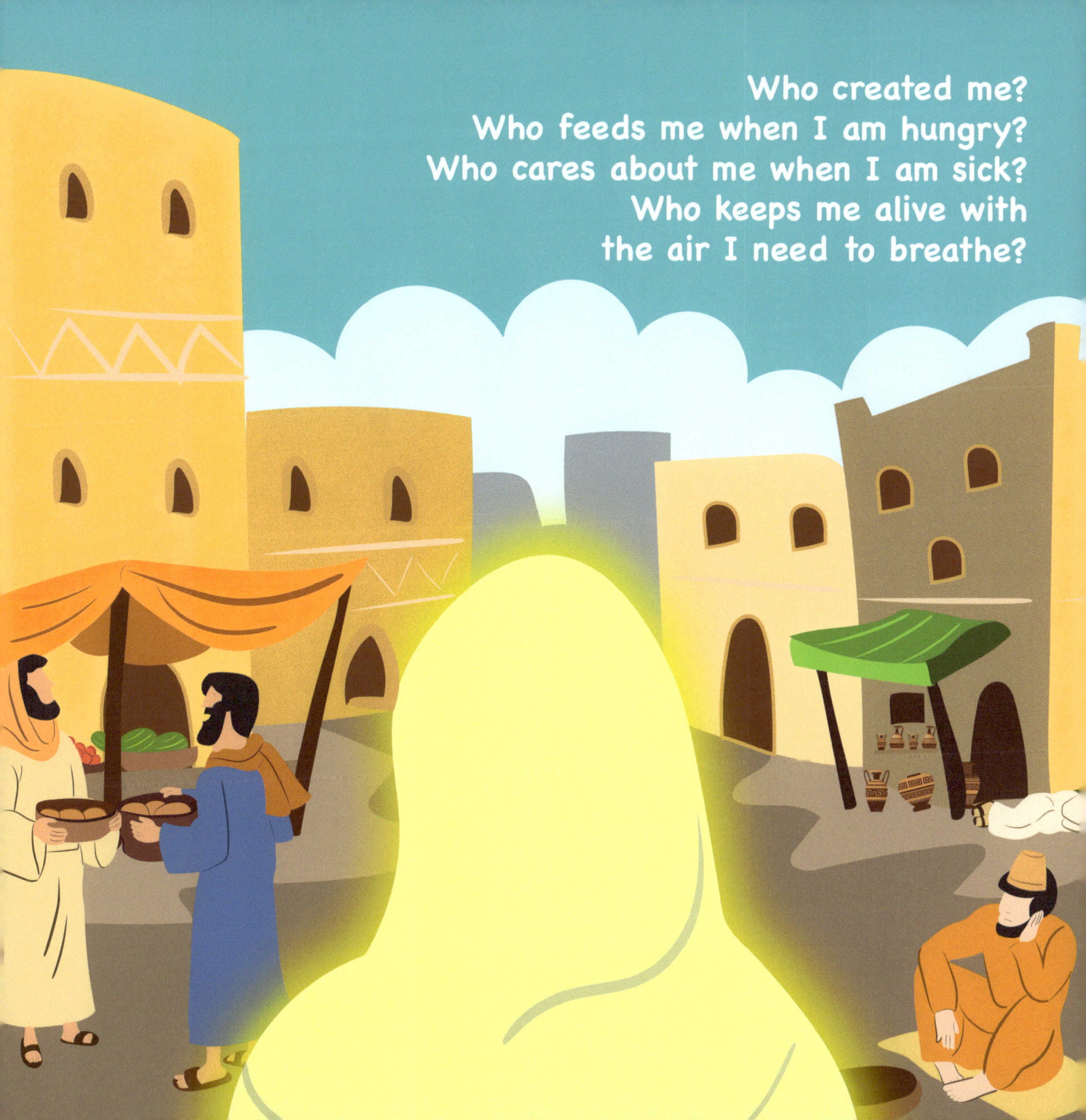

Who created me?
Who feeds me when I am hungry?
Who cares about me when I am sick?
Who keeps me alive with
the air I need to breathe?

Ibrahim (AS) looked
everywhere for answers.
He was continuously searching,
thinking, and looking...
He looked all around him and
did a lot of research!

Finally Ibrahim (AS) came to a decision.
He had found solutions to
all of his questions.
He found the creator of
the STARS, MOON, and SUN...
And of himself!
The creator was God/Allah (SWT)!

Still, today, until the Universe is destroyed
If someone searches...
To try to find God/Allah (SWT)...

They can...
Do research...
Look at their surroundings...
And find God/Allah (SWT).

Allah (SWT) is everywhere!
Allah (SWT) is always active!
Allah (SWT) watches us!
Allah (SWT) sees us!
Allah (SWT) created us!

Allah (SWT) created the whole Universe!

Other great books by Zabed Mohammad!
We hope you like them!

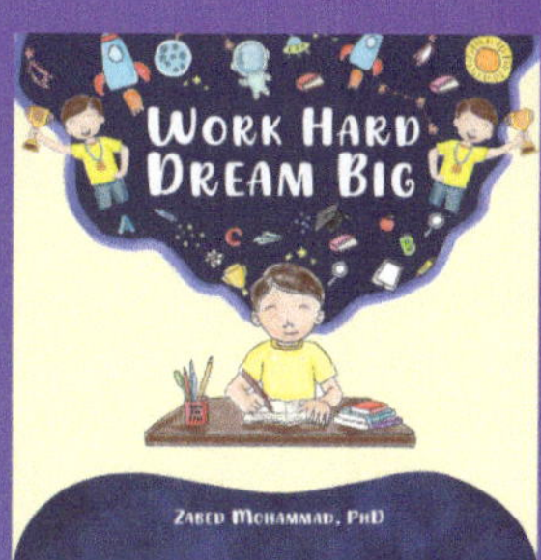

INFO@KIDSEDUCARE.CA
ZABEDM@KIDSEDUCARE.CA